ALTERNATOR BOOKS™

UNEXPLAINED

THE ROSWELL UFO MYSTERY

Craig Boutland

Lerner Publications ◆ Minneapolis

Copyright © 2019 Brown Bear Books Ltd

All rights reserved. International copyright secured. No part of this book may be reproduced, stored in a retrieval system, or transmitted in any form or by any means—electronic, mechanical, photocopying, recording, or otherwise—without the prior written permission of the copyright holder, except for the inclusion of brief quotations in an acknowledged review.

Lerner Publications Company
A division of Lerner Publishing Group, Inc.
241 First Avenue North
Minneapolis, MN 55401 USA

For reading levels and more information, look up this title at www.lernerbooks.com.

Main body text set in Minion Pro.
Font provided by Adobe Systems.

Library of Congress Cataloging-in-Publication Data

Names: Boutland, Craig, author.
Title: The Roswell UFO mystery / Craig Boutland.
Description: Minneapolis, MN : Lerner Publications, [2019] | Series: Unexplained (Alternator books) | Includes bibliographical references and index. | Audience: Age 8–12. | Audience: Grade 4 to 6.
Identifiers: LCCN 2018058301 (print) | LCCN 2018059997 (ebook) | ISBN 9781541562912 (eb pdf) | ISBN 9781541562820 (lb : alk. paper) | ISBN 9781541573802 (pb : alk. paper)
Subjects: LCSH: Unidentified flying objects—Sightings and encounters—New Mexico—Roswell—Juvenile literature.
Classification: LCC TL789.5.N6 (ebook) | LCC TL789.5.N6 B68 2019 (print) | DDC 001.94209789/43—dc23

LC record available at https://lccn.loc.gov/2018058301

Manufactured in the United States of America
1-46408-47498-4/5/2019

Contents

Introduction 4

Finding the Wreckage 6

The Official Story 12

Extraterrestrial Bodies 18

The Real Truth? 24

Glossary 30

Further Information 31

Index 32

Introduction

In the summer of 1947, something strange happened near the town of Roswell, New Mexico, and the Roswell Army Air Field. A local rancher reported finding wreckage from an aircraft that had crashed. What exactly he found is unclear. The air force took away the wreckage before anyone else could see it.

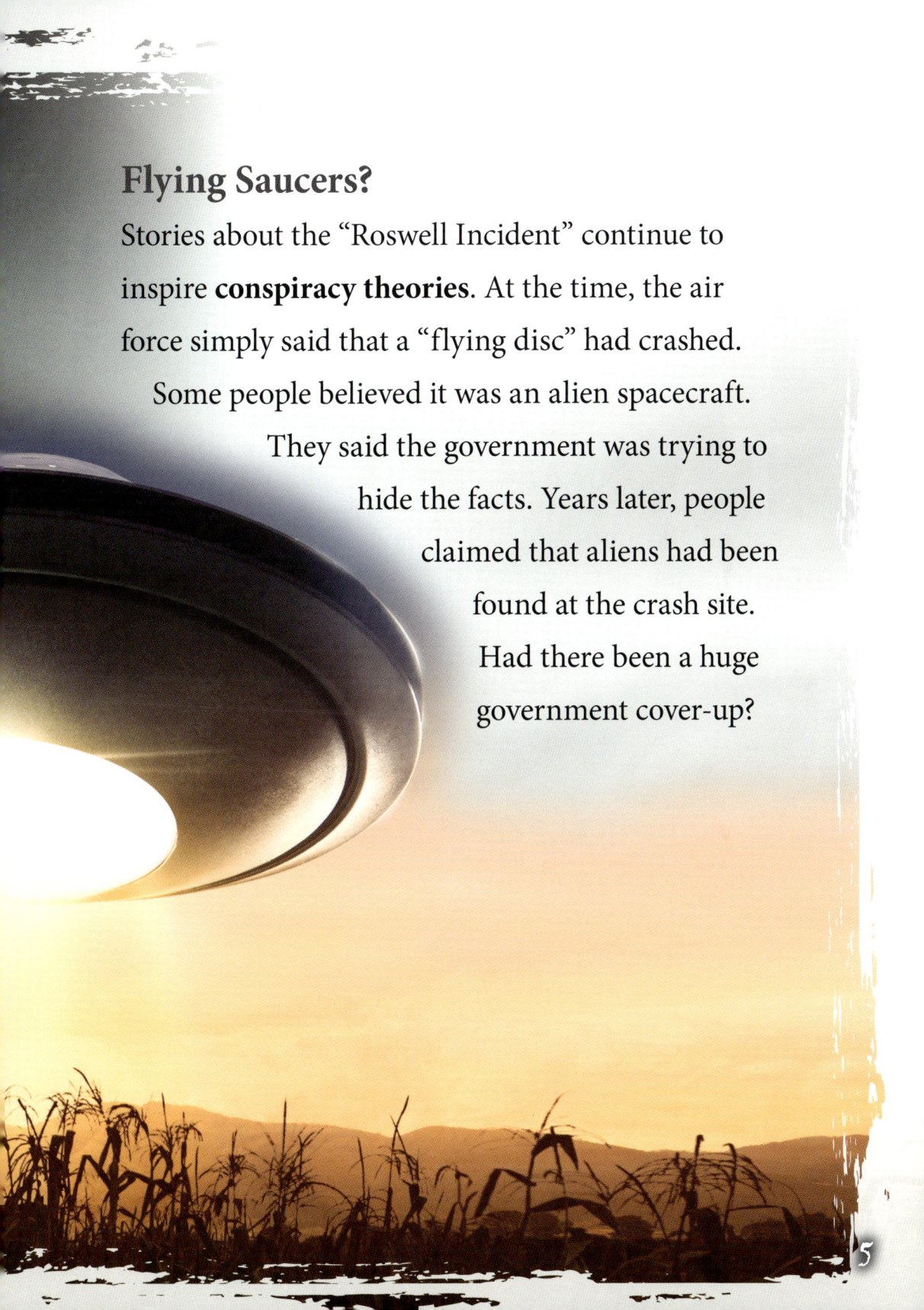

Flying Saucers?

Stories about the "Roswell Incident" continue to inspire **conspiracy theories**. At the time, the air force simply said that a "flying disc" had crashed. Some people believed it was an alien spacecraft. They said the government was trying to hide the facts. Years later, people claimed that aliens had been found at the crash site. Had there been a huge government cover-up?

Finding the Wreckage

In June 1947, rancher William Brazel found some small pieces of some sort of wreckage. He found tinfoil, rubber, paper, and pieces of wood. Brazel talked to some of his neighbors about what he had found. They suggested he take it to the sheriff in the local town of Roswell.

Brazel went into Roswell and showed some of what he had found to the sheriff. The sheriff contacted the local air force base. All the missions flown from the base were secret because the aircraft carried nuclear weapons. Major Jesse Marcel went to Roswell and looked at what the rancher had brought into town. Then he followed Brazel back to the ranch. He collected more pieces of wreckage and took them back to the air force base.

The town of Roswell has become famous for more than dairy farming.

Secret Sites

The Trinity Site was about 120 miles (193 km) from Roswell. This was a secret government area. In 1945 the first **atomic bomb** had been tested there, and the US Army was using the same area to test rockets captured from the Germans during World War II (1939–1945). This was unknown to the citizens of Roswell at the time.

After the wreckage was taken by the army, the air force base issued a **press release** saying that the military had collected a disc found by one of the local ranchers. The press release also said that the disc had landed on the ranch near Roswell sometime in the previous week.

The shield of the army unit in Roswell was a pair of wings on either side of an atomic bomb cloud.

The news that a flying disc had landed in New Mexico immediately caused alarm. The *Roswell Daily Record* newspaper published a headline claiming the military at Roswell Army Air Field had captured a flying saucer. There had been a similar news report a few weeks earlier. In June 1947 Kenneth Arnold, the pilot of a private airplane, was flying over the state of Washington. He reported seeing a flying saucer. Could the Roswell wreckage be from the same alien spaceship?

The front page of the *Roswell Daily Record*, July 8, 1947.

Change of Story

William Brazel thought that the remains were from a flying disc. After Kenneth Arnold's claim to have seen a flying saucer, a reward of $3,000 was offered to anyone finding evidence of flying saucers. Brazel may have gone to the Roswell sheriff to claim the reward. Whatever Brazel had found, the government moved quickly. They put out a story that had nothing to do with a disc or alien spacecraft.

The Official Story

The wreckage of the unidentified flying object (UFO) was examined by airplane experts at the Roswell Army Air Field. After that it was flown to Fort Worth, Texas. Fort Worth was the headquarters of the Eighth Army Air Force. The commanding officer there was Roger Ramey. He invited a group of reporters to a meeting.

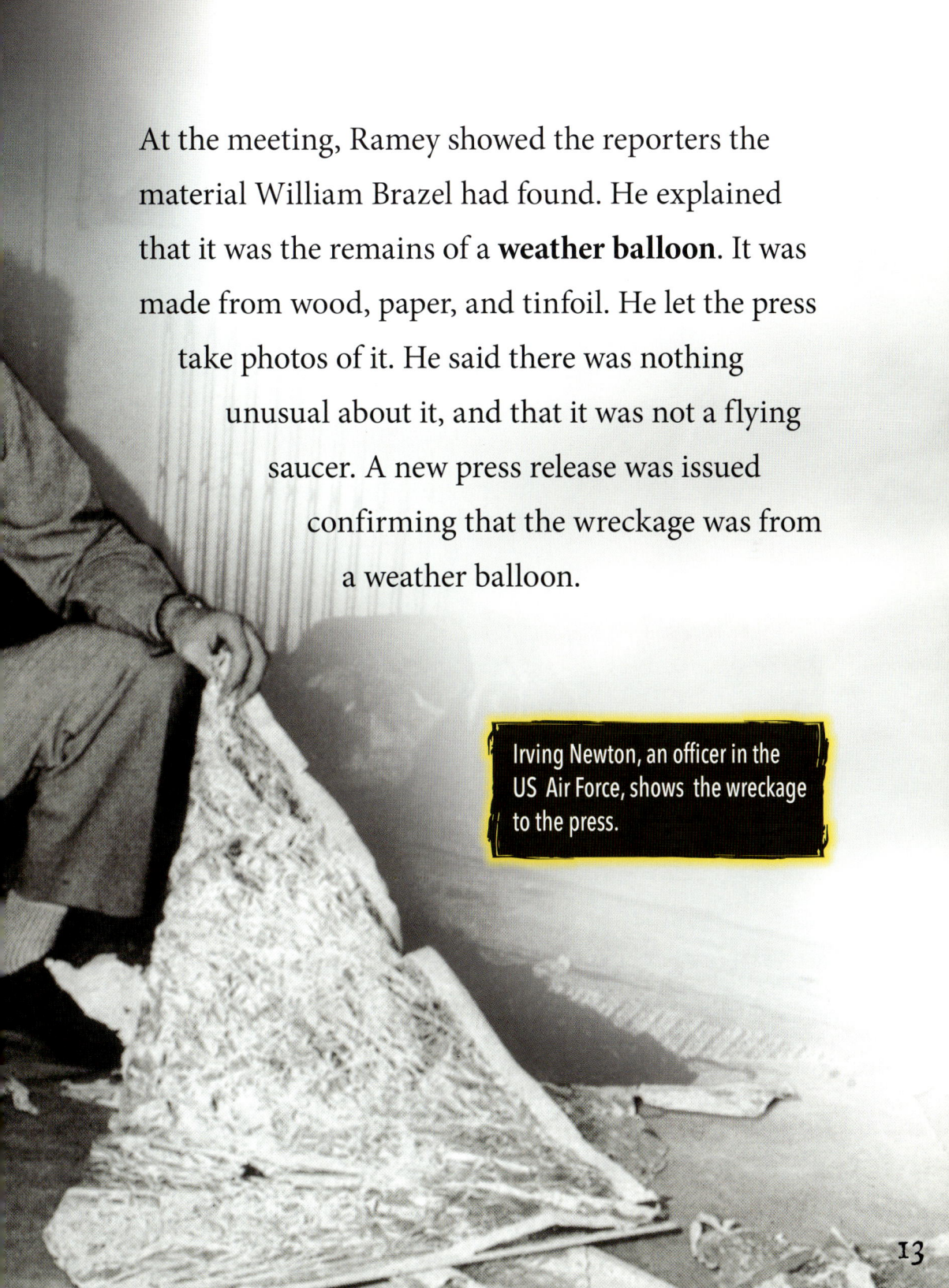

At the meeting, Ramey showed the reporters the material William Brazel had found. He explained that it was the remains of a **weather balloon**. It was made from wood, paper, and tinfoil. He let the press take photos of it. He said there was nothing unusual about it, and that it was not a flying saucer. A new press release was issued confirming that the wreckage was from a weather balloon.

Irving Newton, an officer in the US Air Force, shows the wreckage to the press.

The wreckage collected from Brazel's ranch was taken to a hangar at the Roswell Army Air Field.

Brazel's Description

William Brazel was interviewed by the *Roswell Daily Record* on July 9. He said he had found strips of rubber, pieces of tinfoil, thick paper, and wooden sticks. He described how it was stuck together with tape. This seemed to confirm the explanation that it was a weather balloon. However, Brazel said he had found weather balloons on his ranch before. He said they were not like this one.

Most people believed that a weather balloon had crashed at Roswell. The story disappeared from the front pages of the newspapers. But not everyone was convinced by this explanation. William Brazel's son said his father would not discuss the incident. He said the air force had held his father in **custody** for a week and only released him after he had taken an **oath** of secrecy. His father promised the military that he would not tell anyone any more details about what he had found that day.

Could the description of "tinfoil" have been wrong?

Unusual Materials

The wreckage sent to Fort Worth was almost immediately flown east to a scientific center in Ohio. Some researchers wondered why, if it was just a standard weather balloon. In 1978 two researchers met with Major Jesse Marcel. By then he was retired. He admitted that he thought the wreckage was unusual. It was like nothing else he had seen. The wood was very thin but could not be broken. What had been described as "tinfoil" could not be torn, or even creased.

William Brazel had shown the wreckage to one of his neighbors before taking it to the sheriff in 1947. Brazel's neighbor confirmed that the materials were unusual. It seemed that something more than just a weather balloon had come down. But why was the truth being covered up?

Airmen demonstrate a radar device being attached to a weather balloon at Fort Worth five days after the Roswell incident.

Extraterrestrial Bodies

A book about the Roswell incident was published in 1980. It was based on interviews with Major Jesse Marcel. After the publication, other people came forward to talk about what had happened. Some people claimed that the bodies of aliens had been found at the site. They said the bodies had been taken away for examination.

> There are no photographs of real aliens. People claimed to have seen the bodies of aliens at Roswell. However, many of these stories turned out to be untrue.

Multiple Stories

One of the first eyewitness stories was from Gradey Barnett. He claimed to have seen the bodies of aliens near a crashed spacecraft. But he said the crash site was in the Plains of San Agustin. This is about 150 miles (240 km) west of the Roswell site. Could more than one alien craft have crashed at the same time?

This model in the Roswell Museum is based on descriptions of the aliens some people say were found in 1947.

Another person who talked about aliens was Glenn Dennis. He had been the owner of a funeral home in Roswell in 1947. Dennis said that someone at the Roswell Army Air Field had asked him if he could supply them with small airtight coffins. Soon afterward a nurse friend of his at the base told him she had been at an **autopsy**. The bodies of three small alien beings were examined.

Secret Papers

A group of **ufologists** in the 1980s believed there had been a government cover-up. They said they had proof of a secret committee of scientists, government officials, and military leaders. The evidence was a set of documents called the "MJ-12" papers. They showed that the government knew aliens had crashed in New Mexico in the 1940s.

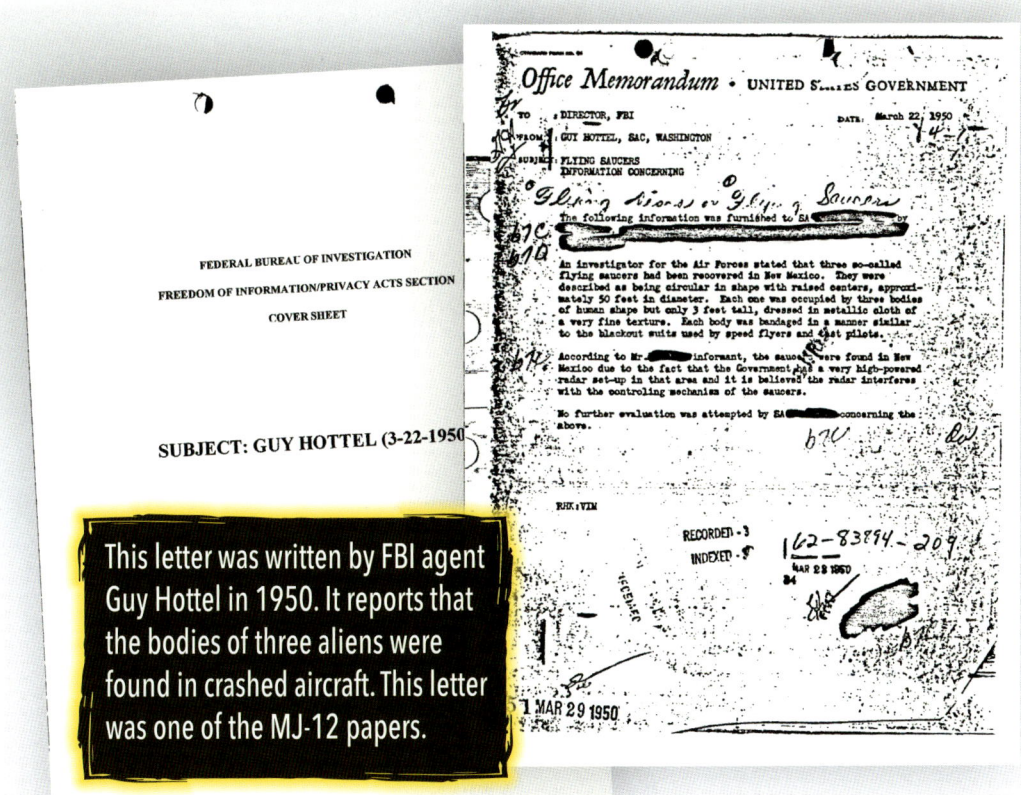

This letter was written by FBI agent Guy Hottel in 1950. It reports that the bodies of three aliens were found in crashed aircraft. This letter was one of the MJ-12 papers.

The most amazing proof that aliens had crashed in Roswell was a film that appeared in the 1990s. It showed doctors performing an autopsy on a small alien being. However, experts discovered that the film was fake. It had been made to look like an old film. All of the stories from people who said they had seen the bodies of aliens are **suspect**. There is no definite proof that the MJ-12 papers are real. Even many ufologists think they are fakes.

Simple Explanation?

Some people say that there were alien bodies found at the Roswell crash site. One possible explanation for this is that they were **crash-test dummies.** These dummies were dropped from weather balloons to see what effects jumping from high altitudes might have on a human body. It would have been too dangerous to carry out such tests using humans. People would not have been very familiar with crash-test dummies in 1947. Perhaps that is what people saw. But what is the real truth about the wreckage at Roswell?

The Real Truth?

There have been many theories about the Roswell UFO mystery since 1947. However, there may be a simple explanation. The incident happened at a time when the United States and the Soviet Union, a nation based in Russia that existed from 1922 to 1991, were struggling for power in Europe.

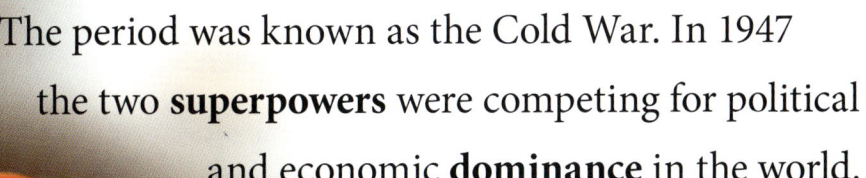

The period was known as the Cold War. In 1947 the two **superpowers** were competing for political and economic **dominance** in the world. The struggle was called the Cold War because the two armies did not fight each other. Instead there was a rivalry between the two countries in a race to develop nuclear weapons.

> In the final year of World War II, nuclear bombs were dropped on the cities of Hiroshima and Nagasaki in Japan. The results were horrific. They are the only nuclear weapons to have been used in the history of warfare. It is thought that the threat of nuclear weapons is enough to prevent future world conflict.

Nuclear missiles can be hidden and launched from underground concrete cylinders called silos.

Spying on the Soviets

In 1946, Stalin, the leader of the Soviet Union, refused to sign a document controlling the use of nuclear weapons. The US increased its development of nuclear weapons in response. It also developed a top-secret **surveillance** program called Project MOGUL. The US wanted to know if the Soviet Union had already tested an atomic bomb.

To do so, the program developed high-altitude balloons. The balloons carried microphones that could detect sound waves from nuclear tests thousands of miles away. The US Air Force was testing balloons at Alamogordo, New Mexico, in June 1947. They lost one of them about 90 miles (145 km) from where Brazel had found wreckage.

Were MOGUL balloons like this one the true explanation for the Roswell mystery and other UFO sightings?

Did William Brazel find a crashed UFO on his ranch in 1947? Was it a secret surveillance balloon? Or perhaps it was simply a weather balloon after all.

The wreckage found at the Roswell site was probably the remains of a balloon—but not a weather balloon. For political reasons, the US government did not want anyone to know the real purpose for the balloon or where it had been. This was why the US Air Force had said it was just a weather balloon.

Do You Believe in Flying Saucers?

Many people continue to believe that aliens crashed near Roswell in 1947. Some people think the government tried to hide the evidence of UFOs and aliens from the public in order to prevent panic. While the government did hide the true purpose of the balloon for a long time, there is no evidence that the wreckage at Roswell was a crashed UFO.

Glossary

atomic bomb: a nuclear weapon that rapidly releases energy, causing damage through heat, force, and radioactivity

autopsy: a medical procedure to find out the cause of death

conspiracy theories: beliefs that official organizations or governments are responsible for unexplained events

crash-test dummies: human-like models of people that are used in experiments that are too dangerous for real people

custody: the imprisonment or protection of somebody

dominance: having power and influence over others

oath: a serious promise

press release: an official statement about a matter of public interest or importance

superpowers: very powerful and influential nations

surveillance: careful observation of something or somebody

suspect: something that cannot be trusted because it is suspicious or fake

ufologists: people who study reports, physical evidence, or other materials relating to UFOs

unidentified: something that is not known or recognized

weather balloon: a large, tough balloon fitted with special equipment that can provide information about the weather

wreckage: fragments of something that has been badly damaged or destroyed

Further Information

Hey Bill Nye, Could the Government Be Hiding Extraterrestrials From Us?
https://bigthink.com/videos/bill-nye-on-alien-sightings-and-government-coverups

Investigating The Truth Behind The Roswell Incident
https://allthatsinteresting.com/roswell-incident

Johnson, C. M. *Close Encounters*. Fremont, CA: Full Tilt Press, 2018.

Kenney, Karen. *Mysterious UFOs and Aliens*. Minneapolis: Lerner Publications, 2017.

Levete, Sarah. *Aliens and UFOs*. New York: Gareth Stevens Publishing, 2017.

National Geographic Video: The Roswell Incident
https://www.nationalgeographic.com.au/videos/secret-history-of-ufos/the-roswell-incident-4483.aspx

What Exactly are UFOs?
https://www.cbc.ca/kidscbc2/the-feed/what-exactly-are-ufos

Williams, Dinah. *UFO Crash Sites*. New York: Bearport Publishing, 2015.

Index

Arnold, Kenneth 10, 11
atomic bomb 8, 9, 26
autopsy 20, 22
Brazel, William 6, 11, 13, 14, 15, 17, 28
Cold War 25
Fort Worth 12, 16, 17
Marcel, Jesse 7, 16, 18
MJ-12 papers 21, 22

nuclear weapons 25, 26
press release 9, 13
project MOGUL 26
Soviet Union 24–26
Trinity Site 8
unidentified flying object (UFO) 12, 24, 27, 28, 29
weather balloon 13–17, 23, 28

Photo Acknowledgments

The images inside this book are used with permission of: ©Shutterstock/donates, p. 1; ©Shutterstock/Fer Gregory, p. 4-5; ©Shutterstock/Laurin Rinder, p. 6-7; ©iStockphoto.com/Extreme Photography, p. 8; © Shutterstock/Victor Maschek, p. 9; ©US Air Force, p. 9 center right; ©Topfoto/Fortean, p. 10; ©Shutterstock/Hurst Photo, p. 11; ©Alamy/Chronicle, p. 12-13; © Topfoto/Fortean, p. 14; ©Shutterstock/Tushatuvango, p. 15; ©Shutterstock, p. 16; ©US Government/UTA, p. 17; ©Shutterstock/Pavel Chagochkin, p. 18-19; ©Shutterstock/photoBeard, p. 20; ©US Government/UFO Casebook/PD, p. 21; ©istockphoto/gremlin, p. 22-23; © iStockphoto/Romolo Tavani, p. 24-25; ©Shutterstock/John Wollwerth, p. 26; ©Topfoto/Fortean, n, p. 27; ©iStockphoto.com/Elvis Fontenot, p. 28; ©iStockphoto.com/MS Cornellus, p. 29.

Front Cover: ©iStockphoto.com/Fer Gregory

Brown Bear Books has made every attempt to contact the copyright holder. If anyone has any information please contact licensing@brownbear.co.uk